In Order

by B.A. Shaver

STECK-VAUGHN

Harcourt Supplemental Publishers

www.steck-vaughn.com

It can be fun to put things in order.
There are many ways to do it.
Have you ever tried?

These people are in an order.
They're in order from oldest to youngest.

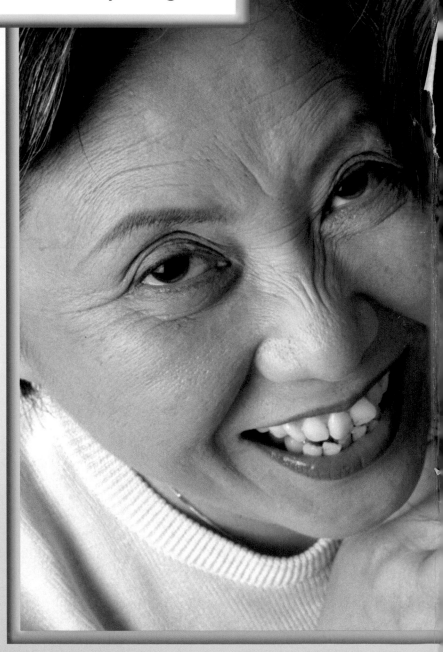

These doors are in another kind of order.
These houses are all on the same street.
Look at the numbers on the door of each house.

The numbers tell where each house is on the street.
Which house has the lowest street number?
Which house has the highest street number?

These animals are in an order.
They are in order from smallest to largest.
The bird is smallest.

The elephant is largest.
Think about your favorite animal.
Where would it go in the size order?

You can put these groups of flowers in an order.
You can order them from fewest to most.
Which group has the fewest flowers?

Which group has the most flowers?
Which group of flowers is in between?
Try pointing to the groups in order.

You can put numbers in an order.
Look at these signs.
They all show numbers.

Can you point to the signs in order?
Order them from the lowest to the highest number.
Don't forget about the numbers in between!

You can also order things by when they happen.
Think about the meals you eat during the day.
Which meal do you usually eat first?

Which meal do you eat next?
Which is usually your last meal of the day?
Can you point to the meals in order?

You can put things in order many different ways.
You can order things from shortest to longest.
Point to the beaks in order from shortest to longest.

Take a close look at these words.
Which word is shortest?
Which word is longest?

You can also put coins in an order.
You can order them by how much they are worth.
Look closely at each coin.

Think about how much money each coin is worth. Then, point to the coin that is worth the least. Order the coins from the least amount of money to the most.

You can order things by how much time they take.
About how long does it take to eat a snack?
About how long does it take to get a night's sleep?

About how long does it take to build a sand castle?
Point to the pictures in order by the amount of time
each task would take.

You can order things from lightest to heaviest, too.
Which object would be easiest to lift?
Which would be the hardest to lift?

Point to the objects in order from lightest to heaviest. Then try ordering them in the opposite way. Order the objects from heaviest to lightest!

These runners will finish the race in order.
Which one will finish first?
Which one will finish second?
Which one will finish third?
Point to each runner in order.
How can you tell who is winning?

There are many ways to put things in order.
How will you put things in order today?